Mekhukhu

South African Institute of Race Relations
Recent Publications

Mauritz Moolman, *From Town to Township: Regional Services Councils Assessed* (1990)

Steven Friedman, *Options for the Future: Government Reform Strategy and Prospects for Structural Change* (1990)

Paul Hendler, *Paths to Power* (1989)

Stanley Mogoba, *A New Africa* (1989)

Stanley Mogoba, John Kane-Berman and Ronnie Bethlehem, *Sanctions and the Alternatives* (2nd edition 1989)

Harry Mashabela and Monty Narsoo, *The Boksburg Boycott* (1989)

Paul Hendler, *Politics on the Home Front* (1989)

Steven Friedman and Monty Narsoo, *A New Mood in Moscow: Soviet Attitudes to South Africa* (1989)

Harry Mashabela, *Fragile Figures: The 1988 PWV Township Elections* (1989)

Harry Mashabela, *Townships of the PWV* (1989)

Paul Hendler, *Urban Policy and Housing* (1988)

Monica Bot, *Training on Separate Tracks* (1988)

Charles Simkins, *The Prisoners of Tradition and the Politics of Nation Building* (1988)

Claire Pickard-Cambridge, *Sharing the Cities: Residential Desegregation in Harare, Windhoek and Mafikeng* (1988)

John Dreijmanis, *The Role of the South African Government in Tertiary Education* (1988)

Chris Heymans, *The Politics of Creation: An Assessment of Government-Created Bodies for Africans in South Africa* (1988)

Chris Heymans, *Akkommodasie sonder Demokrasie: Regerings-liggame vir Swart Politieke Verteenwoordiging in Suid-Africa* (1987)

These are available from:

The Publications Department
South African Institute of Race Relations
P O Box 31044
2017 Braamfontein

Mekhukhu

Urban African Cities of the Future

Harry Mashabela

Senior Research Officer
South African Institute of Race Relations

SOUTH AFRICAN INSTITUTE OF RACE RELATIONS
JOHANNESBURG
1990

This report is published with the financial assistance of the Industry Support Unit in the United States. The unit comprises representatives of American Signatory Companies to the Statement of Principles operating in South Africa.

Published by the South African Institute of Race Relations
Auden House, 68 De Korte Street,
Braamfontein, Johannesburg, 2001 South Africa

PD 11/90
ISBN 0-86982-374-4

Printed by Galvin & Sales, Cape Town

Synopsis

Shack settlements, a consequence of population growth, migration of people from rural to urban areas, inadequate housing and government policy not to provide rented houses, are today a common feature of African township life within South Africa's industrial heartland – the Pretoria/Witwatersrand/Vereeniging (PWV) region. As ordinary folk, who happen to be in the majority, battle to house their families, informal settlements are likely to become the predominant urban African towns or cities of the future. The government must either once again adopt as its policy the provision of rented conventional housing on a large scale or allow informal settlements to develop.

In most of the PWV tin towns, inhabitants have set up a committee, often with the encouragement of such service organisations as the Black Sash and advice centres. But, in most cases, organisation is weak and committees can barely be said to be representative.

Residents complain that the distribution within these settlements of gifts from charitable organisations like the Witwatersrand Council of Churches, Operation Hunger and the Red Cross often gives rise to tension because some committee members allegedly either favour members of their own ethnic group in handing out the donations or sell the articles to make profit for themselves and their families.

Another complaint centres on 'rights' related to trading or running shebeens, tuckshops and the sale of fruit and vegetables. Some committee members tend not to tolerate competition if they themselves are involved in these businesses, according to shack dwellers. Such allegations have, however, been denied by most committee members. But there are individual cases in which residents are known to have risen against corrupt leaders.

In a sense, shack settlements are the flotsam and jetsam of urban African society. They are at the mercy of black local authorities, many of which are alleged to be corrupt. Harassment in the form of shack demolitions, demands for rent payment, and the threat of removals are constant sources of conflict and concern within these settlements.

Sometimes, even the people who rise among shack dwellers to assume the leadership role end up as self-serving individuals, and the wider community's involvement in their plight is also virtually non-existent. Only a few organisations and individuals are known to be actively giving some measure of support to these shack settlements.

In their uncertain, fear-ridden and harassed lives, therefore, the shack dwellers are alone, left entirely to themselves with virtually nobody paying attention to their cries. 'They have become pawns in the political struggle and no consideration is given to their needs and aspirations,' says one of the few community workers who are daily trying to make the life in some shack settlements a little more bearable.

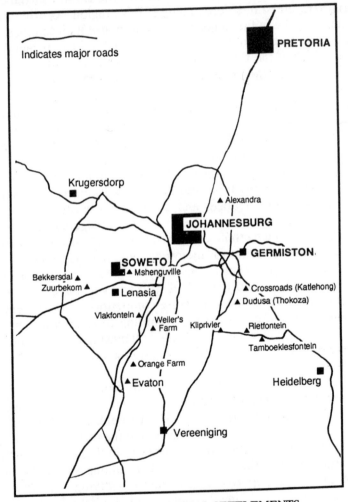

LOCATION OF INFORMAL SETTLEMENTS

Contents

List of Illustrations

Introduction

Rickety tin-and-board dwellings, the result of a chronic housing shortage, are a common feature in every African township in the Pretoria/Witwatersrand/Vereeniging (PWV) area. Though these shacks or informal dwellings were originally limited or confined to backyards, they have now risen in open spaces either within or adjacent to the townships. Some have been erected without authority even on land which does not belong to the local authorities administering the residential areas, as thousands upon thousands of people battle to give shelter to their families.

These informal settlements dramatically reflect the extent of homelessness in the industrial heartland of South Africa. Apart from the shack dwellers on the outskirts of the townships, thousands of homeless people lodge with families living in conventional township dwellings, and in their outhouses and garages. Others live as waifs under bridges and in alleys in the cities of the PWV.

Except for the backyard rooms and garages the shack dwellings are generally called *mekhukhu*, a Sotho word for temporary dwellings, even though the structures may have been standing for years. There is, however, neither a Sotho nor an Nguni word used even by urban Africans to refer to people resident in mekhukhu, because traditionally a mokhukhu (singular for mekhukhu) is considered a mere temporary structure made and used only while the real homestead or house is under construction.

Although the term 'squatters', a word without any equivalent in African languages, is widely used in referring to shack dwellers, its use will be avoided in this study mainly because it conveys a notion of illegality. This sense of the word is often inappropriate, in that many mekhukhu have been put up with official blessing and inhabitants even pay monthly rentals to the relevant black local authorities. The sub-title, *Urban African Cities of the Future*, is intended to reflect the belief that because majority urban Africans are too poor to afford building conventional houses and, in consequence, have to erect mekhukhu even in official resettlement areas, these shantytowns are likely to become cities of tomorrow.

'Shack dwellers' will, therefore, be used throughout the report in preference to 'squatters' to describe the residents who make up these desperate communities.

The object of this study is to look at the problem of homelessness — a problem that has become especially acute since the lifting of restrictions on migration from the designated homelands and from white farms to urban areas. In tackling this problem the government will inevitably have to make deals with the inhabitants of the shack settlements. This study looks at the organisation of these settlements in order to examine exactly with whom the government could negotiate, with specific attention to the following issues:

- whether or not each settlement has set up a committee to attend to its needs as a community;
- how the committee — if it exists — was elected;
- how representative of the settlement the committee is;
- what services the committee provides;
- by whom decisions are made regarding allocations of business rights for vendors such as tuckshops, shebeens, fruit/vegetable stalls;
- how the community reacts to such decisions;
- whether there are any groups or individuals who challenge those who decide;
- what the effects are of the activities of such groups on the life of the settlement; and
- what role political activist community groups or trade unions play in each of these settlements.

I
The rise of shack settlements

Mekhukhu are characterised by an air of desperation and uncertainty, and a culture of poverty. They lack services and amenities. They are the product of both population growth and old government policy which halted provision of housing in urban African areas in an attempt to arrest further African urbanisation. But the urban African population grew despite that policy because of both economic and natural forces.

Mr John Mavuso, Member of the Executive Committee (MEC) in the Transvaal in charge of housing and community development, has said that there are 1,4m Africans living in 'squatter' conditions in the Transvaal alone. About 80% of them live in the PWV region.[1] But his figure of shack dwellers in the Transvaal is far lower than an alternative figure of 2,4m people known to be living in shacks in the PWV region alone.[2] Mr Mavuso also stated that a total of 9 073 families are living in backyards and a further 3 000 in informal settlements in Thokoza, 31 000 families at Katlehong, 5 550 families at Khutsong (Carletonville), and 18 955 in the Sebokeng/Evaton area.[3]

An immediate consequence of population growth and inadequate accommodation was the rise of backyard dwellings. As time went on more and more such structures and garages also were erected by enterprising township residents specifically for renting out to the growing homeless population. Official attempts to get rid of the unsightly shacks not only by razing them, but also through police raids and prosecution of those involved, failed to halt their growth.

When the government introduced the historic 99-year leasehold for Africans in 1978 and thereby accepted their permanence in the urban areas it was the dawn of a new era – an era of hope and promise. The African housing market was opened up and began slowly to be stripped of restrictions. Not only were township residents allowed to put up houses of their own choice, but the wealthier ones could also raise loans from the private sector to do so.

However, as the government freed African housing, it also decided to abandon the task of providing Africans with rented accommodation as it had done prior to the late 1960s. A result of this decision was that only a small number of urban Africans, those in the higher income

11

group – among them professionals, businessmen and public servants (for whom substantial government subsidies were available) – could afford to build houses for their families. On account of poverty and unemployment, the majority could not.

The problem of homelessness was aggravated by the fact that the new black municipalities which were taking over control of the townships from the then administration boards were not financially in a position to provide housing. Another factor that contributed to an increased inflow of people to the urban areas was the repeal of influx control in 1986, which made it possible for migrants who had always wanted to bring their families to the urban areas to do so. The repeal of the pass laws also had the result that families who were unhappy with homeland independence because of the introduction not only of taxes, but also of levies by chiefs, began migrating to towns in the white-designated area.

As a consequence, the problem of homelessness became critical. The result was the growth of massive informal settlements or shantytowns. The fact that registered tenants charged sub-tenants and backyard dwellers monthly rentals (as much as R40 in some cases), also added to the rise in shack settlements as families who resented paying the high rentals fled from the overcrowded homes and backyards to put up their own mekhukhu on vacant land.

Several other factors have been cited as having contributed to the migration of Africans to the PWV region and the resultant increase in homelessness. Speaking in her personal capacity at a conference on housing the poor held at the Centre for Policy Studies, Graduate School of Business Administration, University of the Witwatersrand, on 1 September 1989, Miss Pauline Morris of the Development Bank of Southern Africa said she believed that many persons living in smaller platteland towns which were economically declining were likely to move to places where some work opportunities were available. In addition, she said, large agribusinesses were buying up land, mechanising, and evicting families who might have been living there for generations. Citing the Bronkhorstspruit/Ekangala region, Miss Morris also said that official economic decentralisation programmes were not generating enough job opportunities for the employment of the economically active population living outside the metropolitan areas.

In addition to a lack of finance, the lack of land allocated for African housing is a major constraint which has frustrated attempts to solve the housing problem in the PWV region, if not throughout the country. At the time of writing, a total of 33 000ha of land in the area had been designated for development since 1986, but half of it was said to be unsuitable for housing.[4]

LOCATION OF MAIN SHACK SETTLEMENTS

It is relatively easy to identify shantytowns throughout the PWV region (see map, page vi). Wherever they are – even those situated within conventional townships – they stick out like the proverbial sore thumb.

In Alexandra, north of Johannesburg, there are four distinct shack settlements, one of which is situated near the local cemetery in the valley of the Jukskei River. The township is crammed with shacks in almost every yard or household all along the north side of Selborne Street.

Bekkersdal township in Westonaria on the west Rand is bordered by Silver City, also known as Spooktown, to the north-west; on the east Rand, Etwatwa borders Daveyton on the east side. Thokoza (Alberton) has its own large tin town which stands grimly at the southern end of the township. It is called Dunusa or Phola Park. In Katlehong (Germiston district) lies Crossroads, yet another large shack settlement standing as testimony to the chronic problem of homelessness and the housing backlog within the PWV region.

Soweto has Mshenguville, situated on what used to be the Mofolo golf course. Other big shack settlements in the complex include Chicken Farm, Kliptown shantytown, Mdlaloseville, also known as Chiawelo or Dlamini camp, Protea South – all of them to the south – and the Naledi camp, which is situated below the Merafe rail station alongside the rivulet dividing Tladi and Naledi townships. Mdlaloseville, unlike others, also has a lot of shacks with brick walls, which create an impression of permanence.

Besides these tin towns which stand cheek by jowl with conventional townships, there are those isolated groups of shanties which are situated on land designated for other race groups. These include shanty settlements such as Tamboekiesfontein, Weiler's Farm, Sweetwaters, Vlakfontein, and Lenasia. Tamboekiesfontein is situated alongside the Klip River/Heidelberg national road beyond the Eden Park coloured township on the east Rand; Weiler's Farm lies to the south of Johannesburg just north of Evaton in the Vanderbijlpark district. A stone's throw away is Sweetwaters. Vlakfontein is hidden in the woods

13

alongside the Golden Highway a few kilometres beyond the Sun Valley entertainment resort at Nancefield. The Lenasia tin town is situated between extensions 9 and 10 of the formal Indian township of that name. Several small clusters of tin shack settlements are also found at Grasmere, Ennerdale and Lenasia South on the southern edge of Johannesburg while others are found in Randfontein, Krugersdorp and Roodepoort.

A common feature of all these settlements is their lack of services, water, roads and schools. Except for Mdlaloseville and Mshenguville in Soweto, where some ablution blocks have been provided by the authorities, inhabitants draw water either from neighbouring townships or from hostels, as is the case at Dunusa and Crossroads, or from communal taps. The people of Tamboekiesfontein draw water from a riverbed. For sanitation, chemical lavatories or pit latrines are used.

In some settlements makeshift school buildings have been erected for use by local children, while at Tamboekiesfontein an old farmhouse is used for schooling. Where not even makeshift facilities are available, pupils attend school in the neighbourhood.

GOVERNMENT PLANS TO REHOUSE THE POOR

Also vital to the study are current official attempts to tackle the problem of housing the poor. In this regard, authorities have specifically set aside two areas — **Orange Farm** (north of Evaton) and **Rietfontein** (to the south of Thokoza and Katlehong on the east Rand) — for the resettlement or relocation of families from some of the massive shack settlements within the region.

Originally, 4 300 stands at Orange Farm were planned for the relocation of PWV shack dwellers. Additional land has, however, been added to Orange Farm, bringing the number of sites to 10 300, said an official of the Transvaal Provincial Administration (TPA) in an interview. Aware that even the 10 300 sites, which are still to be surveyed, are inadequate, the TPA has made available another 1 000 fully serviced sites at an adjacent area north of Evaton specifically for the relocation of better-paid shack dwellers from the affected shack settlements.

Of the original 4 300 sites at Orange Farm, 2 000 were for families from Weiler's Farm, 1 000 for those from Mshenguville in Soweto, 219 for people from Alexandra and the rest for shack dwellers from the numerous other settlements in the Lenasia/Grasmere/Ennerdale complex, such as Vlakfontein and Sweetwaters. Often these were people who were left behind with nowhere to go when the farmers for whom they had been working either sold their farms or had them expropriated by the government nearly 15 years ago. It is understood the 6 000 extra sites are to be allocated only to families from Soweto (see Mshenguville under *Case Studies* of this report). By August 1989, 438 shack dwellers from Weiler's Farm were already resettled at Orange Farm and an unspecified number from Soweto and other areas had also moved in.

Situated about 35km south of Johannesburg, Orange Farm has been provided with basic services only: surveyed sites, graded roads and one communal tap for every 30 families. Sites are being sold at R500 each and virtually all the families already resettled there have erected informal houses or shacks for themselves.

In October 1989, a spokesman for the TPA's regional director in Germiston said in an interview that Rietfontein was earmarked for the relocation of shack dwellers from Katlehong, Thokoza and Tamboekiesfontein. Although he said that it comprised only 4 300 sites, Mr Mavuso announced in January 1990 [5] that there were 6 269 surveyed sites, including 80 business stands, at Rietfontein. Only 2 986 of these sites, he added, were already occupied by 4 000 shackdwellers from Tamboekiesfontein, 888 from Thokoza and 983 from Katlehong — a total of 5 871 people.

It would seem as if the establishment of Rietfontein as a resettlement area is only the first phase of a grand development plan by the government intended to link Thokoza, Katlehong and Vosloorus together into one huge black residential area. This is indicated by the fact that the TPA was already talking of more than 6 000 surveyed sites at Rietfontein by January 1990, whereas it said in October 1989 that the area comprised only 4 300 sites. This means that expansion of the new area is under way.

Since August 1989, families have been resettled at Rietfontein. A TPA spokesman said in an interview that residents paid a monthly rent of R45 for 'the land, services and refuse removal'. The only services provided are chemical latrines and water tanks from which residents draw water for their households. The spokesman also explained that families would eventually buy their sites 'once the township has been proclaimed in two years' time'.

The TPA spokesman also said that Rietfontein was part of the

15

southern development of the area and as such might be linked up with Thokoza, Katlehong and Vosloorus. However, he added that it still belonged to the TPA at that time. Responding to questions in Parliament in 1987, Mr Chris Heunis, the then minister of constitutional development and planning, said that Katlehong, Thokoza and Vosloorus would be amalgamated. The area south and east of Katlehong and south and north of Vosloorus up to the proposed K146 road and the N3 throughway would be made available for further expansion, thus consolidating the three townships.[8]

Both Orange Farm and Rietfontein are woefully inadequate, however. Orange Farm is not big enough to house the more than 30 000 homeless at Mshenguville alone, while Rietfontein can accommodate only a fraction of the thousands upon thousands of shack dwellers now resident at Crossroads, Dunusa and at Tamboekiesfontein.

1. Registrations at Orange Farm. When councillor Mr Butana Tshabalala of the Sofasonke Party invited shack dwellers in Soweto in August 1989 to see sites at Orange Farm where they could settle if they wished, they turned out in thousands. And once at Orange Farm, near Evaton south of Johannesburg, they stood in several queues registering.

II
Mekhukhu: seven case studies

1. ALEXANDRA (JOHANNESBURG)

Background

Since the mid-1980s, the whole of Alexandra has been under a vigorous renewal scheme. The redevelopment programme has given rise to numerous backyard tin shacks in virtually every household, particularly along the north side of Selborne Street. In addition there are four distinct shack settlements within the area, which together with the myriad backyard dwellings accommodate the more than 21 000 homeless people resident in the township.

Prior to September 1989, a mysterious organisation called Isolomzi People's Union of South Africa operated in the township. Though lacking organisational structure, it claimed to be a trade union for shack dwellers. Isolomzi (a Xhosa word for home-guard) was charging shack dwellers R5 each per month, supposedly to pay legal fees in the event of eviction from and demolition of shacks. When the Alexandra Civic Organisation (ACO) learnt of these charges, it told residents to stop paying. 'We mean to protect the homeless from sharks, whether they be lawyers or not,' said Mr Moses Mayekiso, chairman of the ACO.

Community Organisation

The ACO established a committee in each of the four shack settlements within the township. Each committee has five elected members, who were inaugurated in September 1989. The committees operate under the umbrella of the ACO and communicate with residents through public meetings.

Mr Mayekiso said that a constitution for the four committees is still being formulated. Functions such as the terms of office for committee members and aims of committees would be embodied in the constitution. Mr Mayekiso explained that the committees were designed to campaign for the provision of facilities and affordable houses for shack dwellers in the township, as well as to resist the removal of residents to other areas.

Future Plans

Originally, the TPA had earmarked 219 sites at Orange Farm near Evaton in the district of Vanderbijlpark for the relocation of shack dwellers from Alexandra, according to Mr Johan Saayman, the local acting superintendent. Mr Saayman stated that families had already been resettled on the sites; but he did not know how many of 6 000 additional Orange Farm sites, which would bring the total number of sites at Orange Farm to 10 300 (see above), would be for families from Alexandra. He said that this decision would be made by the regional office after the land had been surveyed.

Mr Mayekiso, on the other hand, said that shack dwellers in the township were not interested in Orange Farm and that only a 'trickle' was likely to go there. His organisation, which has been negotiating with the Alexandra Council for a better deal for shack dwellers, would like to see affordable houses put up for the homeless on the open land at what is called East Bank extension, where 5 500 sites are available for development. He said: 'We need to have a say regarding the development of the 5 500 sites. We also want to be told who is to develop the area and how much is to be charged. Affordable housing is like a living wage. In considering it, account should be taken of minimum wage levels and the fact that there's lots of unemployment. And it should be done in such a way that it does not affect a person's standard of living.' He also stressed that provision of affordable houses was necessary on the grounds that the whole problem of homelessness was a direct result of government policy. 'We know that the council plans to build a golf course for the people of Alexandra south of East Bank, but to the north of the township. We have already told it that houses should be provided on that piece of ground. This is because we believe that houses are more urgently needed by the people than a golf course,' he said.

Early in November 1989 the ACO bitterly attacked the black local authority for issuing summonses to families with rent arrears. Mr Mayekiso said several families who owed large sums of money (ranging from R2 000 to R4 000) were given three days within which to pay or to defend their action at least in writing. At the same time, Mr Mayekiso warned families who accommodated others in their backyard shacks not

18

to break the long-standing rent boycott by forcing their lodgers to pay. It appears that the Alexandra Council issued the summonses in an attempt to demonstrate its power, possibly hoping thereby to isolate the community organisation. This show of strength on the part of the council probably arose from a previous clash with the ACO. The ACO had been involved in talks with the council concerning the provision of housing in the township, but had abandoned the deliberations after alleging that the local authority was inefficient and corrupt. The ACO then wrote to the TPA, asking for direct discussion with the provincial administration. However, its appeal was refused. Hence the apparent desire on the part of the council to flex its muscles in face of the ACO's attempts to challenge its authority, including its ability to collect rents.

2. CROSSROADS (KATLEHONG)

Background

Katlehong's Crossroads, named after the shack settlement of the same name in the Cape Peninsula which was once a symbol of resistance, is the oldest shantytown in the PWV region. According to residents, the settlement was started in 1982 when a small number of families who were tired of living in congested conditions in backyards erected 90 shacks on an open piece of ground, beyond the railway line on the north side of the township. It rapidly grew into a settlement with a population which is now estimated at over 30 000. In 1988 there were 97 500 homeless people in Katlehong.[1]

Crossroads inhabitants said that they were promised that houses would be erected for them if they participated in the October 1988 municipal elections. To this end they were even taken in two Putco buses free of charge by the then council chairman, Mr Jimmy Tlhagane, and another councillor, to an open space near Vosloorus where, they were assured, their houses would be built. In the end they voted and, as residents of Ward 20 (which consists of Crossroads and Spruitview, one of the prestige suburbs of Katlehong), they are officially represented in the Katlehong Council. However, not only are they still waiting for the erection of the promised houses, but their elected representative, Mr Norman Mukhari, lives outside the settlement, and residents claim that he was last seen in the shantytown on election day in October 1988.

19

Nevertheless the residents' recognition and acceptance of the black local authority is evidenced by the fact that they obtain licences from the council for all businesses (tuckshops, hawking, fruit/vegetable selling) that they operate within the settlement. Shebeens are unauthorised and are run illegally. Residents said that they pay the council R25 monthly in rent for a tuckshop, R15 monthly for selling fruit/ vegetables and R10 monthly for hawking.

Community Organisation

For almost six years after the establishment of Crossroads, residents had a ten-member elected committee, the Crossroads Homeless Committee, which assisted in the running of their affairs and virtually controlled the settlement. Elections for this committee were held every year, and it held regular public meetings with residents. In an attempt to curb crime, the Crossroads Homeless Committee arranged street patrols every evening and encouraged every family to have a whistle. In the event of trouble, the whistle would be blown, calling residents to help the victim. Men, women and children, armed with weapons, would converge on the scene. According to Mrs Rose Ndzimande, an active member of the committee who, despite a limited education, has committed herself to serving the people of Crossroads, any tsotsi or hoodlum caught by the people would be beaten before being taken to the police. 'Through the whistle, residents knew whether they were being called upon to get to a meeting or to give assistance to someone being molested – depending on the sound of the whistle. It was a powerful weapon, this whistle. As a result of our organised street patrols there were no rapes, thefts and common assaults in the settlement,' she claimed.

On Saturdays, refuse removal was organised by the committee: a hole was dug and residents collected the garbage and dumped it into the pit. Mrs Ndzimande also said that fires were common in the tin town, and that whenever a fire or a death occurred, residents reported to her. She then took representatives of affected families to the Witwatersrand Council of Churches (WCC), which usually assisted with food, clothing and blankets. In the event of a death, the church organisation gave R1 500 to the bereaved family to cover funeral expenses (ie a coffin, burial costs and transport). Such help was given particularly in cases where parents were unemployed.

In the early days of the settlement, the committee, assisted by the

Black Sash, installed six latrines with a bucket system for residents while the Red Cross arranged with the army for the provision of water trucks from which families drew their water supply. Alternatively, residents drew water from a hostel for migrant workers some distance away. Another person who assisted the settlement's inhabitants was the late Dr Abu Baker Asvat, who came to the settlement to attend to the sick whenever necessary, and treated them free of charge. 'His death is a terrible blow to us,' said Mrs Ndzimande, who has also established a postal delivery service for residents.

Unfortunately, the authorities took exception to the activities of the committee and to its links with outside service organisations and individuals. The committee was subjected to constant police raids in 1986/87 for allegedly co-operating with the 'comrades' in its street patrols. Then Mrs Ndzimande, who had a licence from the black local authority for the tuckshop she ran in the area, had her tuckshop raided on 15 March 1987. She said that her groceries in the tuckshop (worth R2 000) were confiscated by the municipal police in the presence of the then council chairman, Mr Thami Siluma, and her licence withdrawn. 'The reason was that the mayor said that I spoke too much and was bringing outsiders into the squatter camp,' she said. Her groceries had still not been returned by the middle of the year, when the present writer interviewed her.

The problems of the Crossroads Homeless Committee worsened in 1988 when a division appeared in the committee over the municipal elections for the black local authority. The committee split into two factions after the settlement community's candidate, Mr Zwaye, was rejected by the then council chairman, Mr Tlhagane. He demanded that they accept Mr Mukhari, who was apparent not known in the area, to stand in the election as their candidate; and one member of the committee, Mr Johnson Tisane, broke away and campaigned for Mr Mukhari. These pressures led to the virtual collapse of the committee as a powerful force within Crossroads, with the result that neither meetings nor elections have since been held. According to Mrs Ndzimande, there was no power struggle, but the committee split because some members believed the promise made by councillors that residents would be provided with houses if they supported their candidate, while others did not. Because of constant harassment and intimidation, the committee ceased functioning after the 1988 municipal elections.

In the meantime the harassment of Mrs Ndzimande, a mother of six children, with three grandchildren, continues. Early in June 1989 Mrs Ndzimande was arrested together with two local youths for allegedly driving a stolen car.

She had been called from a funeral service to a scene in the area where some persons were attacking an unknown man whom they accused of kidnapping children. While Mrs Ndzimande was talking to the residents asking them to stop molesting him, the man escaped, leaving his car behind. 'We were still standing there when some policemen arrived. They told me that I would be held responsible if the people burnt the man's vehicle. As I cannot drive I asked two local boys to help me take the car to the police station in Katlehong. A few kilometres outside the settlement we met some police. They stopped us and said we were driving a stolen car. We told them what had happened and that we were taking the car to the police station, but they would not listen. We were arrested,' Mrs Ndzimande said.

By early September — exactly three months later — the case against Mrs Ndzimande and the two boys was still pending. They had appeared in court six times, but charges had not yet been laid against them. The boy who had been driving the car was still in custody while the other boy had been released with a warning. Mrs Ndzimande had, however, been released on the day of their arrest, after paying R100 at the Katlehong Police Station.

Future Plans

Inhabitants of Crossroads are among the people to be resettled at Rietfontein (see above), an open farmland lying to the far south of Katlehong. Removals there started late in August 1989. Mr Tau Molotsi, chairman of the Katlehong Council, said that the 35 000 residents of Crossroads were being resettled at the rate of 50 families every week and he hoped that all shack dwellers in the township, including the Crossroads people, would have been resettled by March 1990.[2] But this is unlikely, because Rietfontein is too small to accommodate shack dwellers not only from Katlehong but also from Thokoza and Tamboekiesfontein.

At Rietfontein, families are charged R45 monthly for services, namely for refuse removal and for water brought in by truck, as there is no water reticulation. A pre-fab creche has also been provided.

Most residents work in Alberton and Germiston. They commute to work by taxi. A single taxi fare from the relocation area to Natalspruit

Hospital is R1,25; from the hospital to Germiston costs R1,30. Thus, the daily return fare for workers with jobs in Germiston is R5,10. A five-day worker must pay R102 a month in taxi fares; a six-day worker R122,40. Most workers are unable to afford these transport costs.

Some residents from Crossroads have already moved to Rietfontein, where at least 'we have peace of mind'. Although Mrs Ndzimande vowed she would 'rather die than go to the new area,' it is feared that because the spirit of her people is virtually broken, she will be isolated and that she might be victimised by the authorities even more than previously.

3. DUNUSA (THOKOZA)

Background

Dunusa or Phola Park, as the tin town is also called, is the largest single shack settlement in Thokoza, a township which had at least 70 000 people known to be living in informal dwellings in 1988.[3] It was established by desperate families in 1987 to the south of the township after the council had demolished their shacks at Sites 1 and 2.

Its origins were recounted by Mr Prince Mhlambi, who is a co-director of Kwasa Community Programmes (Kwasa), a community-based organisation which, together with the local Roman Catholic Church, gives assistance to shack dwellers. He said that about 150 families, who were living in shacks at the coalyards (Site 1) and paid rent to the coalyard owners, were ordered off the land by the council, because the land had been sold to a private developer. Their shacks were subsequently demolished on 22 July 1987, and for two weeks these families remained in the open at the coalyards. During this time one person died and a woman gave birth. According to Mr Mhlambi the Witwatersrand Council of Churches (WCC) gave them tents. Some of the shack dwellers eventually trekked to the garbage dump near the local water tank (Site 2) and pitched their tents amid the rubbish. Those who remained at the coalyards did so largely because they had no money to pay for the removal of their belongings.

In the meantime, the Red Cross supplied blankets to all families, in addition to negotiating with the council on behalf of the shack dwellers for a place where they could settle. The council said that they could settle at Site 3, but only if they put up tents and not tin shacks. The families at Site 2 objected to this restriction, and turned down the council's offer at a public meeting, where a committee was elected, with Mr Caiphus Ndlela Mabindisa as chairman, to fight for a better deal. However, those families which had remained at Site 1 agreed to move to the new area.

Mr Mabindisa was given additional blankets by the Red Cross to distribute among the homeless, to whom he sold the blankets instead. His actions angered residents, particularly those who knew the blankets were being donated free of charge. He subsequently died when shack dwellers attacked him and burnt his shack.

In the end the people at Site 2 also moved to Site 3. Contrary to the wishes of the council, however, they erected shacks, and more and more homeless families joined them there. In 1989 the population of Site 3 was estimated at more than 30 000.[4] Residents named their shantytown Dunusa, which literally means 'behave rudely, with your backside up'.

Needless to say, the shack dwellers of Thokoza and their leaders view service and welfare organisations such as the Red Cross and the WCC with gratitude. They said that without the relief these bodies give, particularly in the form of blankets and tents, their condition would be utterly unbearable.

Another community leader, Mr Paul Ngobeni, a businessman who is also chairman of the Thokoza Residents Unity, a local civic organisation unaffiliated to any political movement, contended that shack dwellers have been given a raw deal not only by the council but also by their own leaders. He said that in the October 1988 municipal elections, the shack dwellers backed two candidates, both of whom were campaigning against monthly levies. These two candidates were duly elected, owing to strong support from the shack dwellers. One became chairman of the council and the other, chairman of the management committee — both positions of influence. Ngobeni said that 'once the two men were in the council, they forgot the cries of shack dwellers. They started putting pressure on these people to pay increased monthly charges of R20'.

Like most other settlements, Dunusa lacks basic necessities such as water, lavatories, health facilities and schools. Residents draw water from a nearby men's hostel for migrants. Until May 1989, 28 chemical latrines were made available to residents. The latrines had been hired by the Red Cross at a cost of R14 800 a month, according to Mr Mhlambi of Kwasa Community Programmes. The Thokoza Council removed garbage from the settlement, but started demanding R50 monthly in service charges. Only some of the families paid, generally out of fear that their shacks would be destroyed if they did not heed the demand.

During July 1989, the people of Dunusa had a running battle with the black local authority as a result of its demand for rent payments. They were raided by the municipal police and had their tin shacks pulled down on numerous occasions; but residents rebuilt their shacks after each demolition. By the beginning of September, the TPA had started to remove shack dwellers from Dunusa to Rietfontein, with no visible resistance from the community.

Community Organisation

According to residents, Dunusa is divided into 12 sections. The settlement has a 30-member committee which attends to disputes among residents, including allegations of assault. It also arranges evening patrols within the settlement in a bid to curb crime. During one of these patrols, on 4 November 1989, one of the committee members, Mr Themba Mayaphi, died violently when they were attacked by alleged vigilantes – people who did not even live in the area. It is not clear whether the vigilantes saw the committee members as a threat or merely wanted to frighten residents out of the area to Rietfontein, the relocation area.

In addition to this committee, the independent Kwasa Community Programmes (Kwasa) of Mr Mhlambi, Christina Thibedi and Blessing Cebisa functions in Dunusa. Kwasa enjoys the support of the local Roman Catholic Church and appears to be the most active organisation in the area. According to Mr Mhlambi, it was started by concerned Thokoza residents. Its work complements that of the residents' committee. Mr Mhlambi said that Kwasa not only encouraged and created self-help projects in shack settlements, but also promoted public awareness, especially in church and business circles, about the conditions under which homeless people live.

Kwasa 'co-ordinates activities of the homeless communities in the Thokoza/Katlehong areas. It is accountable to the community through its committee, which is made up of 21 members, of whom two are from each of the nine projects run by the organisation. In addition, there are three other members – two directors and a co-ordinator'. The two directors are Ms Thibedi and Mr Mhlambi, while Mr Cebisa is the co-ordinator.

The organisation's activities in the settlement include the running of literacy classes and of two creches; it advises residents on basic issues such as pensions, and blue cards for unemployment insurance fund claims; it runs 13 soup kitchens which feed on average 1 300 children a day; and there are nine trained women who teach 32 others basic sewing skills, material for which has been provided by the Roman Catholic Church.

Attempts by the Isolomzi People's Union to operate in the settlement were frustrated when its leader, who had been living there with his family, was thrown out by residents in May 1989. According to residents, the reason for this was that the 'activities of his organisation were not in the interest of the community. It was exploiting the homeless'.

Future Plans

The TPA says that, like the community of Crossroads in nearby Katlehong, the people are to be resettled at Rietfontein. Some have been moved already. While service charges at Rietfontein are slightly lower than at Dunusa (R45 and R50 respectively), transport costs are higher: monthly taxi fares for those working a five-day week in Germiston amount to R102 and for a six-day week to R122,40, while monthly fares from Dunusa (Thokoza) to Germiston amount to R52 for those working a five-day week and R62,40 for a six-day week.

4. MSHENGUVILLE (SOWETO)

Background

When Mr Ephraim Tshabalala, a Soweto businessman who was then chairman of the Soweto Council, allowed some homeless families to settle on the piece of land he owned near his Eyethu cinema and also on a portion of the Mofolo golf course in 1986, he could not have foreseen that he was starting the largest single shack settlement within the vast complex of Soweto. Within weeks, more and more families who had been living in backyards moved in there — and also on to land other than that owned by Mr Tshabalala — without permission from the council. The families paid Mr Tshabalala R35 a month, apparently for permission to erect shacks there and for the provision of chemical latrines. However, they paid directly to the council after his resignation as a councillor.

Although the black local authority first tried to move the people from Mshenguville, it eventually gave up, apparently for fear of provoking violent resistance and also because there was no alternative accommodation. The shack settlement grew to large proportions in two years, despite official attempts to restrict its growth. In 1988 it consisted of 31 254 jampacked tin dwellings.[5] Calculated at an average of five persons to a shack, the population would then have stood at 156 270, a figure which excludes the top portion of the golf course alongside Roodeport Road, which was still vacant at the time.

Surrounded by neat brick-walled houses and now occupying the entire golf course, the jumble of tin and cardboard shacks is situated in Mofolo in the heart of Soweto. It is overcrowded, squalid and ugly; yet it is also vibrant and irrepressible in its own sordid way.

Not surprisingly, many inhabitants of Mshenguville express their allegiance to the Sofasonke Party and to its president Mr Tshabalala, whose clan name is Mshengu and after whom the tin town was named. The fact that he resigned from the council in November 1986, in protest after the police and the army bulldozed some of the dwellings and teargassed residents, must have enhanced his image as a leader within the settlement.

The Sofasonke Party has fared well in council elections in Soweto because of the support from the homeless who live in the area and mistakenly believe that the party will provide them with houses. As a party, Sofasonke has no authority to build houses which residents can rent. Many a candidate who won an election on a Sofasonke Party ticket but then turned his back on the party became a casualty in subsequent elections.

According to residents, Mshenguville has been divided into nine zones by councillors, and families pay to the council a monthly rent of R35. The tin shacks lean virtually one against the other, with a mere passage between them. The settlement lacks streets and roads, and most other facilities; although Dr Johan van der Westhuizen (public relations officer of the Soweto council) said in an interview that 198 chemical latrines, two ablution blocks and numerous water taps had been provided. Garbage piles up in every nook and cranny in the settlement, and a smell of poverty permeates the shantytown. Local children who attend school do so outside the area. Shebeens abound,

27

as do fruit and vegetable stalls, in the battle to survive within the squalid settlement.

Community Organisation

Attempts by outside agencies, among them students from the University of the Witwatersrand and representatives of the Black Sash, to help Mshenguville residents form committees appear to have been unsuccessful. Even block committees which residents said once existed are now said to be inoperative. It appears that this failure is mainly due to the heavy reliance of shack dwellers on the Sofasonke Party and the Tshabalala family to represent their interests, as this party has a proven record of having championed the cause of the homeless within the area.

When officials began resettling families from Mshenguville at Orange Farm in August 1989 a new voice arose in the form of the hitherto silent and obscure youth league of the Sofasonke Party. This group publicly denounced the move to resettle residents, and a spokesman cited 'lack of schools, shortage of water and sewerage facilities' in the new area as reasons why the majority of residents were against removal. He also claimed that the Sofasonke Party leadership had promised families that they would be resettled either at Zuurbekom or in Krugersdorp.[6] But the pronouncements of the youth league conflict with the overwhelming response of Mshenguville shack dwellers when invited by the party and the local authority to tour Orange Farm on Sunday 6 August 1989. This excursion was to facilitate registration for those families wishing to resettle.

In addition, on 13 November 1989 a group, which called itself Masakhane Mshenguville Squatters Committee and claimed support from local residents and people from Evaton, Sebokeng and Tembisa, tried to hold a march to Mr Ephraim Tshabalala's house to protest against the removal. The march was, however, disrupted by the police.[7] Indications are that this so-called squatters' committee was not in fact a local group. Masakhane, for instance, is the Weiler's Farm committee which is resisting the removal of families from there to Orange Farm. Another pointer is the claim to support coming from as far afield as Evaton and Sebokeng, let alone Tembisa on the east Rand.

It seems likely that the Sofasonke Party youth league sought help from groups in other areas which were also opposed to removal, and together quickly formed the Masakhane Mshenguville Squatters

Committee specifically to whip up anti-removal feeling within the settlement. But the league's attempt to discourage residents from going to Orange Farm appears to have been unsuccessful.

Another organisation, the Domestic Workers Association, has been battling (with scant success) since the early days of the shantytown's existence to do community work, including running literacy classes in the area. Ms Nana Moabi, co-ordinator of the association's project, said in an interview that 'because of the economic climate which has resulted in lots of husbands' being unemployed, our intention is, among other things, to alleviate poverty in the home by giving some skills to women and helping them form co-operatives through which they can get materials cheaper and generate some income. No sooner had Mshenguville been established in 1986 than we moved into the area. We held discussions with local women, telling them of our intentions and they welcomed the project. However, it never took off. Each time we went in to meet a group, we found new faces despite previous arrangements, which meant beginning all over again'.

Future Plans

It is the intention of both the TPA and the black local authority to resettle Mshenguville inhabitants at Orange Farm near Evaton. Earlier in 1989, for example, Mr Sam Mkwanazi, the mayor of Soweto, announced that more than 30 000 Mshenguville residents would be resettled at Orange Farm and also at Zuurbekom, which is situated on the western outskirts of Soweto.[8] Originally, only 1 000 stands at Orange Farm were earmarked for the people from the shack settlement. But Dr Van der Westhuizen said that, as far as he knew, all the 6 000 additional stands which have been allocated to Orange Farm would be made available for people from Soweto. These 6 000 sites, he added, were still being surveyed, and he hoped that the first lot would be ready early in 1990 for families to be resettled. It is clear, however, that even with the 6 000 additional sites, the new resettlement area remains inadequate.

A stand (150 square metres) at Orange Farm costs R500 and monthly service charges are R24,50, which is R10,50 less than families pay at Mshenguville. Furthermore, sites are rentfree. But, predictably, transport costs are high: a single busfare from the area to Johannesburg is R2, while the taxi fare is R3, which means that workers have to pay R6 a day if they commute by taxi and R4 if they use the bus.

5. TAMBOEKIESFONTEIN

Background

Tamboekiesfontein, an open piece of land broken into two sections by the Klip River/Heidelberg road, is a private farm which originally belonged to the late Mr Naas Louis Ridley, a coloured man and veteran of the Second World War. When his wife entered an old age home the farm was divided among four individuals: Messrs Johannes Gaboo, Casper Williams, Louis Moses and Mrs Irene Vertein. During 1988, each of the four households allowed homeless families to erect shacks on their individual holdings after payment of between R40 and R60 for a site, plus a monthly rental ranging from R10 to R20.

These families were mainly from Thokoza and Katlehong where, they said, they were harassed by police raids on shack settlements and backyard dwellings. Having fled the townships, they became the original residents of the shack settlement at Tamboekiesfontein.

Once word got round that sites were available for homeless families at Tamboekies, as residents commonly refer to the settlement, it expanded rapidly. But as the settlement grew, it also attracted the attention of the Peri-Urban Areas Health Board and the TPA. The landowners were charged early in May 1989 and prosecuted at the Heidelberg Magistrate's Court for allowing outsiders to settle there without permission. By November 1989, the case against them was still in progress.

In June 1989, the regional office of the TPA issued an undated notice to the community in which it stated that all the people living at Tamboekiesfontein or intending to move there should take note of the following:

- rumours that the government will provide free housing to people who live at Tamboekiesfontein are untrue, false and misleading;
- at no stage will the government provide free housing, for nowhere in the world does any government provide free housing. All people have to provide their own houses;
- the situation at Tamboekiesfontein is a serious health hazard and if more people move here, it will become worse; and
- it is illegal to squat at Tamboekiesfontein, and people living there would probably be forced by the so-called landlords and landladies to make illegal payments to them while they could have saved that money to pay for a decent home elsewhere.

The conflict between the landowners and the authorities resulted in defiance among some of the men already settled there. They allowed friends and relations to move in, without paying anything to the landowners, according to Mr Williams.

This state of affairs was complicated by the fact that the four landowners had begun fighting among themselves after the authorities acted against them. They no longer worked together. A committee they had formed in February 1989, with Mr Davis Shai as secretary/rent-collector, was disbanded as a result of the in-fighting. The committee had been established to attend to the needs of the settlement.

Community Organisation

Tamboekiesfontein as a community is in disarray, owing to disagreements among the four landowners, and because the committee has ceased to function. The Tamboekiesfontein committee had been formed by the landowners (excluding Mr Gaboo) to administer the area, to collect rent from residents, to arrange a transport service for residents, to settle individual disputes and to operate as a burial society. The committee was disbanded after the chairman, Mr Simon Mashinini, stopped the secretary from collecting rent from shack dwellers.

Mr Shai, the secretary, had been appointed to collect rent in sections B, C and D, which belong to Mr Williams, Mr Moses and Mrs Vertein respectively. Mr Gaboo had been acting independently, which implies that a division among the landowners existed even before the authorities stepped in.

When a public meeting was held in the settlement to discuss the question of the committee, all stayed away except the people resident in Section B. Early in September, the bloodied bodies of two people (a man and a woman) who stayed in Section B and had been out drinking the previous evening, were found in the open veld nearby, beaten to death, and so the previously muted conflict burst into the open.

There is no water in the settlement. Residents draw the water they drink and use in their homes from a nearby riverbed. Mr Williams has dug a borehole alongside his homestead for his people in Section B but, apparently because of a lack of funds, machinery to enable families to draw the water has not yet been installed. Schoolchildren either attend classes in an old farm house or go to institutions outside the area, as no proper facilities are available within the settlement.

Future Plans

As a settlement, Tamboekiesfontein is doomed. Inhabitants are to be relocated at Rietfontein, a few kilometres away, where they will be obliged to pay monthly rentals of R45. However, not all the people are likely to be removed because Rietfontein as it stands cannot cope, considering that it serves as a resettlement centre for residents of Crossroads and Dunusa as well. Additional land will have to be found if all the shack dwellers are to be relocated.

6. VLAKFONTEIN

Background

Vlakfontein was established in 1986 as a shack settlement, and by July 1989 it consisted of about 600 tin shacks. The settlement is situated in the woods about 4km beyond the Fun Valley entertainment centre in Nancefield on the Golden Highway. Because it lies in a wooded area it is not easily visible from the national road.

The settlement lies in an area officially designated for Indians. Unlike its counterparts elsewhere in the PWV area, such as Mshenguville, Crossroads and Dunusa, it is airy and relatively pleasant. Its residents hail from local farms, from the homelands, particularly the Transkei, Bophuthatswana, QwaQwa and Venda, as well as from Malawi, according to Mr Jabulani Mkhize, the local community leader.

Mr Mkhize said: 'If someone comes along looking for a site to put up his own shack, we tell him we have the authority neither to give him a place nor to refuse him the right to stay here. It all depends on the individual; whether he is prepared to take the risk or not. If he is prepared, then we ask him to look for a plot where he can erect his own shack in our midst. And there is no charge whatsoever. It is entirely free.'

With the assistance of Operation Hunger, the people of Vlakfontein have been able to establish a creche/preschool and a feeding scheme for children. But they have no water in the settlement, even though Mr Mkhize claims that that is no problem as 'we get water from Indian households in the neighbourhood'. The shack dwellers have had three boreholes dug, but they are not yet in use, as the community 'is still trying to get equipment'.

Vlakfontein, like other shack settlements, teems with shebeens, spaza or tuck shops, and fruit and vegetable stalls. In an attempt to keep the shantytown clean, residents have dug holes into which they dump all the rubbish. Every family has to dig its own pit latrine.

Community Organisation

In 1987 Vlakfontein inhabitants elected a 12-member committee, with Mr Mkhize, who had been the community leader and spokeman since the creation of the settlement, as chairman. It was the duty of the committee to attend to the needs of the community and settle whatever disputes and conflicts might arise. The committee then divided the settlement into six sections to facilitate administration.

Mr Mkhize said that it was by sheer accident that he had the leadership of Vlakfontein thrust upon him. When the Peri-Urban Areas Health Board issued notices to families in 1986 to dismantle their shacks, he took the initiative and sought outside help. 'I didn't really know exactly what to do to resist removal of the settlement. For days, I stayed away from work. I approached both Dr Abu Baker Asvat and the Black Sash and told them what was happening to us. Dr Asvat immediately gave us tents as temporary shelter for those families whose shacks had already been demolished by the officials. Through the Black Sash we got legal representation and the threatened removal ended. I was then picked up by the people as their leader and this has to date remained so', he said.

After Mr Mkhize lost his job in the process, he asked residents to choose someone else in his place so that he could seek employment, which they refused. Instead, they decided to contribute 50c a family towards a monthly salary, in order to enable him to attend full time to the problems of the community. As more money was raised than he needed for his family, he decided to apply for a post box for residents at the Grasmere post office.

He also tried to start a feeding scheme but Operation Hunger, whom he approached for help, told him that he first had to erect a kitchen. Unfortunately, he said, 'the money I had was neither enough to put up the structure nor to pay those who would be needed to cook'. Operation Hunger did, however, agree to supply mealiemeal and soup, and residents contributed building material for the erection of the kitchen. The feeding scheme began and the kitchen structure, a mere tin shack, also served as a creche/preschool. However, it turned out to be too small for this purpose, as there were too many children. Operation Hunger again came to their rescue by donating building materials to erect a bigger and better corrugated iron structure for a preschool.

Four young women in the community volunteered not only to cook but also to tend the children. Feeling that the four women should be paid for their efforts, Mr Mkhize called a public meeting and told residents of his predicament regarding their payment. At the meeting, it was decided to increase the 50c contribution to R2 a family, and in January 1989 the contribution was again raised from R2 to R10 monthly.

Contributions were made to individual committee members in the various sections, and receipts were issued for every payment, according to Mr Mkhize. Although these funds were supposed to be handed over to the committee's office at Mr Mkhize's home, which is situated in the same yard as the preschool, he said in an interview in July that some committee members were no longer bringing in the contributions. He said that at first he 'thought this was on account of unemployment even though I wondered why they were not informing us of the problem. But then I started hearing stories that they claimed we were embezzling the money. I immediately called a public meeting to look into the problem. It was decided that those who did not co-operate should be driven out of the settlement. We as a committee have not carried out that decision. We are in fact reluctant to do so. Instead we feel that we would refuse to settle disputes or family problems of those refusing to co-operate'.

With regard to businesses, Mr Mkhize explained that any person in the settlement who is interested in establishing a business can do so: 'However, we do want them to let the committee know in advance. Some do in fact inform us, but others do not. We don't interfere with them even if they do not tell us in advance because we feel that they are doing a great deal of service as there is a lot of unemployment'.

When considering the fact that the way the local committee runs the settlement is somewhat decentralised, with individual committee members given the task not only of collecting levies, but also of settling disputes among residents in the sections in which they live, Vlakfontein seems more democratic than most of its counterparts elsewhere in the PWV region. Other evidence of democratic principles is the fact that communication is maintained on a regular basis between residents and the committee regarding decisions and the resolution of problems.

Future Plans

Residents of Vlakfontein are destined for resettlement at Orange Farm, about 15km away. According to community leader Mr Mkhize the shack settlement residents do not want to go to Orange Farm because 'we ourselves are running Vlakfontein. Whatever the government wants to do for us, we want them to do it here, nowhere else'. In addition, families would be expected to pay R500 each for a site at Orange Farm.

United resistance to resettlement may be threatened by the fact that there is already a rift among residents over payment of contributions towards the running of the creche/preschool in the shack settlement. It is possible that those refusing to pay may accept removal, and so weaken whatever resistance the committee may have wanted to mount.

Besides, there is the issue of non-payment of levies by some committee members who, it was resolved, would be expelled from the settlement – though the committee has been reluctant to kick them out. Conflict over this issue threatens to split residents into rival factions, and such a division would very likely be exploited by the authorities in implementing their removal plans.

7. WEILER'S FARM

Background

Weiler's Farm is situated about 35km south of Johannesburg, in the Grasmere area. The two Weiler brothers who owned the farm resisted its expropriation by the government, and allowed homeless families to stay there for as long as they paid rent – in defiance of government policy.

When the two brothers eventually abandoned the struggle to retain their farm and moved to Johannesburg in 1985, the shack settlement population had grown from 300 in 1983 to about 1 500 persons. By 1987, this figure had risen to 12 997, despite regular police raids and arrests.[9]

According to residents, the growing shack settlement assumed a new status in 1987 when it was declared an emergency camp, and a superintendent was appointed by the provincial administrator to administer the area. Residents were, in terms of the emergency camp regulations, issued with permits authorising their stay there by the superintendent.[10]

A residents' committee, the Weiler's Farm emergency camp committee, was also established after the settlement was declared an emergency camp. In addition, the settlement was divided into ten wards, and for the first time, families had to pay a monthly rent of R35. Water was and is still drawn from taps.

Another consequence of the declaration of Weiler's Farm as an emergency camp was the erection of a prefab administration office for the superintendent, with an adjoining office for the police, at the entrance to the shack settlement. Residential and lodger permits are obtainable from this office.

In 1989, Weiler's Farm had a preschool and a primary school, both of which are run by the committee. The primary school caters for children from substandard A right up to standard 7. Residents said that the preschool was established in 1987 with 150 children, while the primary school was established the following year with a total of 929 pupils and 15 teachers. By the end of that year, however, the primary school population had decreased to 679 pupils, either because their parents had sent them to schools outside the settlement or because they had dropped out of school altogether.

Initially, World Vision paid salaries to the three childminders at the preschool and also provided feeding for the children, while equipment was donated by the Australian embassy, according to community leader and committee member Miss Olga Lutu. The settlement is not entirely dependent on outside financial help, however, as parents have to 'make small contributions' if their children are at the schools.

Community Organisation

As already indicated, Weiler's Farm has been divided into 10 wards. Residents in each ward were asked by the superintendent to nominate two representatives to the committee, which thus comprises 20 members. However, Miss Lutu said in August 1989 that six of the 20 members of the committee had left the area, and that no new nominations had been made. According to the emergency camp regulations, the committee serves as a liaison body between the superintendent and the inhabitants. Its role entails making recommendations to the superintendent in respect of 'any matter relating to the interests of residents'. Disagreements between the committee and the superintendent have to be referred to the regional director for a decision or ruling.

The administrator may dismiss a member if he thinks that person's continued membership of the committee 'directly or indirectly may disturb the peace and good order in the camp or obstruct the exercise of the powers or functions or duties of the committee'. The administrator can also dissolve the whole committee if he feels that its continued existence may lead to the disturbance of peace and order in the camp, or if he feels that it has failed to perform any of its functions and duties.

It is noteworthy that the declaration of the settlement as an emergency camp, which resulted in the introduction of the R35 service charge, split the community into two factions. Some were opposed to the idea of paying a service charge when there were 'no services being rendered other than the water which was and is drawn from taps', said residents.

As a result of the division, only the Weiler's Farm emergency camp committee (the Weiler's Farm residents committee headed by Miss Lutu) is co-operating with the TPA while another – the Masakhane committee – operates in opposition to the provincial administration. This committee was formed by residents who felt that the new committee would not serve their interests. Mr Geoff Budlender, director of the Legal Resources Centre in Johannesburg, who has handled several cases in the area, said that the committee established at Weiler's Farm after the shack settlement was declared an emergency camp was 'to have no executive powers, but would only represent the residents in dealings with officials'. He also said that the committee had achieved a good deal, but added that its position had increasingly come under attack, because it was seen by some as the agent of the TPA, rather than as the agent of the settlement community.[11]

The emergency camp committee which had been holding monthly meetings with the TPA officials in 1986, prior to Weiler's Farm being declared an emergency camp, advised residents to pay the required service charge. According to Miss Lutu, the committee advised them to pay because 'after being arrested some lost their jobs or risked losing them. During this period of conflict some residents lost confidence in our committee and we experienced division for the first time in our history. The division was a direct result of the implementation of the emergency camp regulations. A group, it was called Masakhane, began operating in opposition. It became very strong at one time'.

Masakhane was established by Mr Monde Dyantyi, who was representing Ward F in the old residents' committee at the time. The group was supported mainly by those families who refused to pay the service charges. Another group opposed to the removal to Orange Farm, led by Mr Silas Lamola and Mr Charles Senyane, a former chairman of the original informal committee, subsequently broke away too.

Mr Senyane, however, moved out to Orange Farm early in 1989, where he was given a site from which he sells coal. Similarly, according to the minutes of the Weiler's Farm emergency camp committee meeting of 22 August 1989, Mr Lamola, a former teacher at Weiler's Farm primary school, applied to the committee for permission to establish a preschool at Orange Farm. His application, made on 7 August 1989, was rejected outright.

If anything, the moves by Mr Lamola and Mr Senyane show just how weak resistance to the removal will be and demonstrates the lack of common purpose among residents, even among those in opposition to official policy. In the conditions prevailing in many mekhukhu, it is difficult for residents to maintain community spirit rather than serving their own individual interests.

Miss Lutu has been accused by her detractors of being used by the TPA to serve their interests and they allege that the TPA has given her one of the large farmhouses at Orange Farm. In response to these allegations she said: 'The farmhouse was not just given to me. I applied for it because it has a telephone and I needed a telephone. In addition, I applied for two residential sites at Orange Farm. Both the two sites and the farmhouse have been granted to me. I applied for the two residential sites because I want to remain within the community and keep in close contact. Our community offices will be at the farm house which will also be made available for use by doctors in attending to the sick.'

Miss Lutu continued: 'Together with my committee, we have informed residents about these developments. This was in June 1989 and the community felt that the Weiler's Farm clinic which was started in my house could continue operating there until a proper clinic is established. Another thing, I need some privacy and the farmhouse will be ideal for that. Our people have accepted all these developments.'

Miss Lutu believes that the relocation area is so close to Weiler's Farm that opposition to moving there is pointless; and that residents have more to gain by settling in the new place than by trying to put up resistance.

Future Plans

Shack dwellers from Weiler's Farm are being resettled at Orange Farm, and in May 1989 the Weiler's Farm residents' committee proposed that the monies levied for services be credited to individual families towards the purchase of sites at Orange Farm, according to Miss Lutu. Sites at Orange Farm, measuring 11 by 26 square metres, are priced at R500 while bigger sites cost R2,27 more for each additional square metre.

The Weiler's Farm emergency camp committee has since its establishment negotiated with the TPA on behalf of residents, not only for a better financial deal in the new area, but also to try and resettle residents as a community so that individual families remain neighbours. As a result, the shack dwellers have been given their own area in Orange Farm, comprising 2 000 sites.

They have also been promised sites for three schools and three creches, as well as three parks for recreation. Business sites, which can either be sold or rented to prospective traders, are also planned. The TPA has, according to Miss Lutu, also agreed to reduce the monthly service charge to R24,47 for those who have bought sites at Orange Farm and to R29,25 for families who are not buying land. She explained that the provincial administration had agreed to reduce the levies on condition that members of the black local authority would receive no monthly allowances when a council is established in the new area.

Miss Lutu said that the TPA had also agreed that residents would be allowed to run informal businesses if they so wished at their homes in Orange Farm in an attempt to fight unemployment, and they would be allowed to erect whatever structures they could afford for their families, even mud houses. No rented housing would be available and the government should not be expected to provide housing. She also said that families could, if they wished, rear animals.

One communal tap will be provided for every 30 families at Orange Farm. Electricity and a sewerage system are to be 'provided in the course of time' but, for the present, families are being encouraged to dig pit latrines which, hopefully, are to be replaced eventually with flush lavatories. The emergency camp committee has successfully negotiated with World Vision to erect creche/preschool structures at Orange Farm. Three schools are to be built with funds provided by private donors.

2. *Vlakfontein settlement. In the woods alongside the Golden Highway beyond Fun Valley at Nancefield lies the Vlakfontein shack settlement, which, unlike most other settlements, is airy with open dirt roads crisscrossing the area.*

3. *Dunusa crèche. In some shack settlements in the PWV area inhabitants have established structures where working mothers can leave their children under the care of child minders, usually elderly women, when going to work. The picture was taken at Dunusa, but could easily have been taken at Vlakfontein or Weiler's Farm where similar makeshift crèches exist.*

III
Shack settlements and organisation

In each of the shack settlements inhabitants have set up a committee to attend to their needs and problems, sometimes with the encouragement, according to residents, of service organisations like the Black Sash and independent advice centres (ie centres not run by the Witwatersrand Council of Churches). Some committees have been established by individuals thrust into the leadership role by sheer force of circumstance. With the exception of the committees at Crossroads (Katlehong) and Alexandra, elections of committee members are seldom if ever held. Members are usually chosen because they were recommended by individual residents, either on the basis of an apparent commitment to work for the community, or their outspokenness at meetings within and outside the settlement. Once in the committee, it seems, a member remains in this position until he himself loses interest or falls into disfavour – an event which sometimes splits the committee into factions.

At the Crossroads settlement, a committee was elected every year; but no committee elections have been held since the 1988 municipal elections. According to former committee members, the elections ended because of constant municipal police harassment. The committee was accused by the black local authority and the police of co-operating or working with the 'comrades'. Anti-crime street patrols which were mounted by the committee were also stopped because of alleged harassment.

In certain cases committees have established creches, feeding schemes for young children and makeshift schools, with assistance from service organisations such as Operation Hunger, the Red Cross, the Witwatersrand Council of Churches, and World Vision. Committees also see to it that the settlements are kept clean and, where possible, arrange for the supply of chemical lavatories to residents.

Attempts at controlling crime, settling disputes, and monitoring the establishment of shebeens, spaza shops, and fruit and vegetable stalls, have also become the responsibility of committees in some cases. New families who want to erect their own shacks within the settlements seldom do so without consulting the committee. At Tamboekiesfontein families seeking sites are permitted to settle on payment of R40. Thereafter, families said they paid R10 each in monthly rent. Although spokesmen of the committees in most other settlements said that they allocated sites to new families free of charge, Mr Ditaba Masupa, chairman of the committee at Hlatheni, a tiny shack settlement at Lenasia South or 'Daxina', as the extension is also called, said that his committee charged a R2 fee to allocate a site to a family. The money was for a common fund for the committee, he explained. It was used for transport to meetings with service organisations in Johannesburg and for burials. Inhabitants, he added, buried their dead either at Avalon in Soweto or at the cemetery in Evaton.

In virtually every settlement, organisation is palpably weak, division in leadership is rife, and committees can barely be said to be representative in most cases. There are complaints in some circles that the distribution of gifts from such service organisations as the Red Cross, Operation Hunger, and the Witwatersrand Council of Churches often give rise to tension within settlements, because some committee members allegedly favour members of their own ethnic group in handing out the donations. Another complaint is that some leaders withhold articles donated by such service bodies for distribution among the needy and sell them. Yet another problem hinges on 'rights' related to trading or running shebeens. Residents said that some committee members suppress competition in business if they themselves are involved in the same business. This applies especially in the case of shebeens, spaza shops, and fruit and vegetable stalls. Such allegations have, however, been denied by most committees.

There are isolated cases in which residents have risen against corrupt leaders. In Thokoza, for instance, committee chairman Mr Caiphus Ndlela Mabindisa died violently when the community attacked him. He was accused of having continued to sell blankets donated by the Red Cross despite objections.

At Katlehong, shack dwellers who want to run spaza shops have to apply to the local authority for a licence to do so, but even here shebeens abound without authorisation. Elsewhere, prospective traders deal directly with their committees.

INVOLVEMENT BY OUTSIDERS IN SHACK SETTLEMENTS

The wider community's involvement in shack settlement is virtually non-existent as only a few organisations and individuals are known to be actively providing some measure of support to shack dwellers in the PWV region. When Dr Abu Asvat was fatally shot on 27 January 1989, shack dwellers were deprived of a generous helping hand. In several shack settlements, members of committees talked glowingly of the treatment and medicine he freely gave to the sick. Although Dr Asvat lived in Lenasia and had a surgery in Soweto, his humanitarian services among the homeless extended as far afield as Crossroads in Katlehong. He has, however, left behind a group called the Imbeleleko Women's Organisation, which provides mobile clinics for shack dwellers at Tsakane, also in the east Rand.

Then there is a group of young folk at Thokoza who, together with the padre of the local Roman Catholic Church, are trying to make life among the people of Dunusa a little more bearable. The group, which goes by the name of Kwasa Community Programmes and is run by the youthful Prince Mhlambi and Christina Thibedi, has established day centres for working mothers at Dunusa and intends spreading its activities.

Shack settlements represent the flotsam and jetsam of urban African society. They are at the mercy of black local authorities (some of which are alleged to be corrupt), and are largely dependent on their whims and fancies. Harassment in the form of shack demolitions, demands by these local authorities for rent, and the threat of removals are constant sources of anxiety within the shack settlements.

In their uncertain, fear-ridden and harassed lives, the shack dwellers are alone, ignored by the outside world. According to Mr Mhlambi of Kwasa, 'homeless communities tend to receive very little of the funding and skills assistance which are available'. He added that 'most of the funding and skills assistance is given to higher profile projects in the cities while the shack settlements lack minimum financial resources to provide basic necessities. Not only are these communities poor, but they also lack a literate leadership to cope with the ever-present threats of removal and demolition of their shacks. They have become pawns in the political struggle and no consideration is given to their needs and aspirations. People talk a lot about them, but do very little – if at all – for them'.

Except for the few service organisations mentioned, society seems to shun the wretched shack dwellers. Though their plight is collective, each man must fight a lonely battle to survive. Even activist political groups ignore their cries. Not even trade unions, which have shown keen interest in housing for African workers (see Hendler P, *Urban Policy and Housing*, South African Institute of Race Relations, pp31-32), pay attention to the plight of shack dwellers. Trade unions and activist bodies alike appear to see the desperate homeless people as the responsibility of church and welfare organisations. Trade unions seem to fear that involvement could tie workers down and so frustrate their union activism, and they also generally regard the provision of housing for Africans as being the sole responsibility of the government.

Mr Chris Dlamini, a vice-president of the Congress of South African Trade Unions (COSATU), said that as an organisation the congress was not assisting shack dwellers in their fight for conventional housing although some members were doing so in their individual capacity in some townships.

Only the ACO, which is led by a trade unionist, has made it its business to identify itself with shack dwellers. Not only has the ACO been instrumental in the creation of the four shack settlement committees in the township of Alexandra but it has also taken them under its wing. As the committees have only recently been established by the ACO, it remains to be seen how democratic and effective they will be.

ACO chairman Mr Moses Mayekiso, who is also general secretary of the National Union of Metalworkers of South Africa (NUMSA), explained in an interview that he is involved in the shack settlements in the township in his capacity as a local community leader and not as a trade unionist. It would be problematic for him to act in his capacity as a NUMSA representative for he would then be expected to seek a mandate from the union.

The ACO's close association with the local shack settlements has boosted morale among the inhabitants. The ACO is not only campaigning for the erection in the township of 'affordable' houses, but also rejects the proposed removal of shack dwellers from the area to Orange Farm near Evaton to the south of Johannesburg. Mr Mayekiso said that his organisation wanted shack-dwellers to be provided with facilities right there in the township.'There are 5 500 open sites at East Bank extension on the other side of Jukskei River which have been earmarked for development. We would like to see affordable houses put up in this area for the shack dwellers.' The ACO would also want to be involved whenever developers are contracted to build houses in the township, in order to monitor the quality and cost of new housing.

Significantly, the ACO does not merely talk of giving support to shack dwellers: it has become directly involved on their behalf, through negotiations with the black local authority and by organising protest marches within the township to attempt to highlight the housing problem.

Regarding removals or the relocation of shack dwellers, the government has said that nobody is forced to move, and that individual families are relocated in approved areas only if they so wish. The fact is, however, that the pressure of raids and demolitions forces shack dwellers to move – as shown in recent months at Dunusa in Thokoza and at Tembisa, where the people were left in the open after the destruction of their shacks.

There are also official inducements through which families are encouraged to accept relocation. Service charges are, for instance, relatively lower in resettlement areas than in existing shantytowns, as is the cost of serviced sites and services. Water, schools and graded roads are more readily available in relocation areas while they are largely lacking in shack settlements.

In January 1989, for example, a notice was issued to shack dwellers in settlements in the southern parts of Johannesburg, which said: 'You can move to Orange Farm now, but only have to start paying the monthly charges for the site from 1 July 1989. This is a special concession to enable you to save money and establish yourself on the new site.' It also told residents that to move to Orange Farm 'ensures you of a permanent residence' and that they 'can own the land'.

Until recently, Isolomzi People's Union of South Africa, which claimed to be a 'trade union for shack dwellers countrywide', had been active in shack settlements in the PWV region. It charged a R35 joining fee, with a subsequent monthly R5 membership fee, and also boasted a housing division which was supposed to be involved in procuring sites for needy members and developing them at a price. However, both the organisation and its housing division, the Mazibambane Housing Project, have collapsed because shack dwellers were suspicious of them and rejected them.

In spite of this collapse, the leading personality in Isolomzi has re-emerged in Vulindlela United Community, a newly formed organisation which claims to serve the interests of shack dwellers.[1] It remains to be seen, though, whether Vulindlela (a Xhosa word meaning 'open the way') will indeed work in the interests of the desperate people living in shack settlements.

In the meantime, the shack dweller, down and out, left to fend for himself without support from either community or trade union bodies, finds the misery and loneliness of homelessness unendurable. He or she is forever looking for an escape, a way out and is thereby exposed to unmitigated swindling by fly-by-night developers – people who exploit his desperation by pretending that they will build him a home, only to vanish into thin air once they have received payment.

SHACK SETTLEMENTS AS CENTRES OF RESISTANCE

It is often argued in some circles that the poor have nothing to lose but everything to gain in resolutely resisting authority; that in this context concerted resistance can only force the hand of those in authority to provide formal housing for the thousands upon thousands now living in shacks. But the assertion is at best a half truth, for the success of such resistance is dependent on a number of factors, chief among them being the support the resisters get from the wider community and the availability of leadership with organisational skills.

Take, for example, the growth of Soweto. Historically, the complex rose to be the colossus it is mainly because of resistance against the Johannesburg municipality, if not the government itself. True, it is a product of community resistance – even defiance; but it might have failed without the initiative of the Sofasonke Party under the strong leadership of the late James Mpanza, who encouraged the homeless to put up a huge shantytown alongside the spruit dividing Orlando East from what is now Orlando West.

The Sofasonke Party, a civic organisation which was formed by Mr Mpanza, who lived in a rented house in Orlando East, spearheaded the fight for provision of houses and thus enjoyed the support of the many families who were without accommodation. By actively identifying itself with the affected people, the civic body gave them the moral sustenance they sorely needed and in turn they invariably enabled civic leader Mpanza and his supporters to win the advisory board elections in which they stood as candidates – even against well-known organisations such as the African National Congress and the Communist Party in the 1930s and 1940s.

Similarly, the people of Crossroads in the Cape Peninsula succeeded for quite some time in refusing to move off the land they occupied without authority. They succeeded, that is, until they split down the middle as a community when one faction started to co-operate with officials who wanted to implement government removal plans. The rift was widened by the in-fighting then prevailing among rival black political groups as they moved into the area and vied to exploit the situation, and gain control of the community.

In other words, only through collective, united action, including support from the wider community, can the poor claim with a measure of certainty that 'they have nothing to lose, but everything to gain' in the struggle for a better deal. Alive to this fact, the PWV authorities have chosen to attack only one shack settlement at a time (or even only part of a settlement), in order to avoid arousing widespread public anger and reaction. Deprived of support from the wider community, and often from the rest of his own community, the shack dweller lives in constant fear, overwhelmed by feelings of insecurity and helplessness.

Often the authorities demolish the relatively new shacks in a settlement, usually a small number, leaving in place those considered to have been in existence for some time. As a result, divisions are sometimes created even among the shack dwellers themselves, with those who have been in the area for a longer time resenting new arrivals, who might attract the attention of officials and thereby threaten the survival of the settlement.

Backyard shack dwellers feel almost as insecure as their counterparts in the shantytowns. Their unhappiness stems mainly from the high monthly rentals charged by the families accommodating them, and their dependence on the daily mood of the heads of the respective families whose backyards and garages they occupy. In consequence, they are just as vulnerable and just as keen to acquire their own home as those living within shack settlements.

It is therefore not really surprising that, even though most of the desperate shack dwellers publicly insist that they will not move out of the shack settlements unless alternative formal housing is provided for them, they almost always seem ready to accept relocation under similar conditions elsewhere. Witness the overwhelming response of the inhabitants of Soweto's shantytown when invited to view sites at Orange Farm near Evaton, about 45km from Soweto. The invitation was issued by Mr Butana Tshabalala, chairman of the Soweto Council's management committee and son of business tycoon Ephraim

Tshabalala, president of the Sofasonke Party. The sortie was to take place on Sunday 6 August 1989, and young Tshabalala had hired 25 buses to convey interested parties to the relocation area. However, so many people turned up at the departure point, Eyethu cinema, that the buses had to run a shuttle service between the cinema and Orange Farm, from 10am to 1pm.

It is noteworthy that representatives of various activist political groups in the Soweto complex failed to turn up at the Eyethu cinema on that day. By appearing, they might have gauged the feelings of the homeless; but their absence illustrates their indifference to the plight of the shack dwellers. Nor did the press, which had announced Mr Tshabalala's call to the homeless, come to report on the response to the invitation.

Once at Orange Farm, some of the people complained when they were belatedly told by young Mr Tshabalala that the available sites were only for those resident at Mshenguville. They felt that they were being left out. Others claimed that living in the new area would be too expensive mainly because of transport costs.

However, relocation is going ahead fairly smoothly, largely because resettled families feel more secure: 'At least I have peace of mind here. Nobody bothers me because the site belongs to me.' As a consequence of the removals to Orange Farm, however, a new problem has arisen: new families move into Mshenguville as others are removed, because they believe that they may get a chance of being resettled in some approved area in the region one day only if they are resident at Mshenguville.

IV
Conclusion

All but a few of the main shack settlements in the PWV have established committee structures to attend to their basic needs, including resolution of disputes, settling petty thefts, and crime control within their communities. The few exceptions are shack settlements in Soweto, near Bekkersdal on the west Rand, and those at Tamboekiesfontein on the east Rand.

In Soweto, rather than creating their own structures, shack dwellers tend to rely on the Sofasonke Party, in the belief that it is the one organisation that may help them. At Bekkersdal, shack dwellers seem to have merged with the rest of the township community to such an extent that they do not consider themselves, nor are they considered by others, a separate entity which would need separate structures of its own.

The committee at Tamboekiesfontein was created not by shack dwellers but by the landowners, who are now fighting among themselves in the face of a protracted prosecution brought against them by the peri-urban authorities. This dispute between the landowners and the authorities has resulted in another conflict: a clash between the landowners and the residents, since some residents either refuse to pay rent or charge new families they themselves bring into the area and pocket the money instead of handing it over to the landlords.

At Weiler's Farm, the emergency camp committee has already assumed an official status that makes it different from the others. It serves as a link between shack dwellers and the TPA, acting in an advisory capacity, in the same way as advisory boards and Urban Bantu Councils functioned.

Whether they be weak or strong, the committees appointed in the shantytowns generally serve to make life a little more bearable for the shack dwellers; though clearly the more powerful bodies such as the ACO, the Crossroads Homeless Committee and the Vlakfontein Residents Committee can achieve more, by holding discussions with the government on how to tackle the housing problem. Where residents have not formed viable structures or where the community is divided into factions, the authorities could lessen tensions by bringing together and talking to the leaders of the various factions or to those groups that enjoy majority support – as at Weiler's Farm.

In the main, the major problem facing these communities lies in the fact that the wider community, including political activist organisations and trade unions, appears to ignore them – with the exception of the ACO in Alexandra. If such organisations and trade unions were interested, they could assist in the development of the leadership skills and organisational prowess which are wanting in most shack settlements. In addition, a sense that the wider communities around them were aware of their plight and concerned about it, would give shack dwellers the moral support they need in their fight against shack demolitions, service charges even where no services are provided, and unwanted 'voluntary' removals.

It stands to reason that it will not be wise for outsiders to move into shack settlements and create structures for the people living there. Such a move is bound to fail, mainly because it does not involve residents themselves in the creation of the necessary structures. The idea should be to help the shack dwellers to create the necessary structures themselves, and to teach them skills such as how to run such structures democratically, as in the settlement of Vlakfontein.

If the shack dwellers are not encouraged to build the structures themselves, they risk the loss of what little independence remains to them. This is already discernible in certain settlements, where many look to service agencies such as the Black Sash and the Witwatersrand Council of Churches to do things for them instead of making efforts to do things for themselves.

It is important not only that the wider community identifies itself with the desperate shack dwellers, but also that the government reverts to its former policy of providing rented homes for the poor if we are to attempt to resolve the problem of homelessness now gnawing at the heart of black urban communities. If the government, for financial reasons, is unable to house the poor, it should then embrace the erection of informal housing as its official policy. This is important because, whether we like it or not, the creation of shack settlements will increase, making such settlements urban African towns or cities of the future, because the poor – the people who cannot afford to build conventional houses – are in the majority.

4. Dunusa stall. A makeshift fruit and vegetable stall is a common feature in all shack settlements within the PWV area. This picture was taken at Dunusa in Thokoza.

5. A tent town. Time and again welfare agencies such as the Red Cross and the Witwatersrand Council of Churches come to the rescue with tents for families whose shacks have been destroyed by local authorities, leaving them in the open.

References

I The rise of shack settlements

1 *The Star* 27 October 1989
2 *Race Relations Survey* 1989/90, South African Institute of Race Relations, p162
3 *The Star* 27 October 1989
4 Cosser E, *Social and Economic Update* 8, South African Institute of Race Relations, March–July 1989
5 *The Star* 10 January 1990
6 Mashabela H, *Townships of the PWV*, South African Institute of Race Relations, 1988

II Mekhukhu: seven case studies

1 Mashabela H, *Townships of the PWV*, South African Institute of Race Relations, 1988, p97
2 *Sowetan* 10 November 1989
3 Mashabela H, *Townships of the PWV*, South African Institute of Race Relations, 1988, p161
4 *The Star* 6 June 1989
5 Mashabela H, *Townships of the PWV*, South African Institute of Race Relations, 1988, p148
6 *The Star* 18 August 1989
7 Ibid 14 November 1989
8 *Sowetan* 14 April 1989
9 Budlender G, 'Urban Land Issues in the 1980s: The View From Weiler's Farm', unpublished paper delivered at a conference at the University of Cape Town, 18 April 1989
10 Board Notice 85 of 1987, *Government Gazette* 31 December 1987
11 Budlender G, op cit

III Shack settlements and organisation

1 *Sowetan* 19 December 1989

References

I The rise of shack settlements

1 *The Star* 27 October 1989

2 *Race Relations Survey* 1989/90, South African Institute of Race Relations, p162

3 *The Star* 27 October 1989

4 Cosser E, *Social and Economic Update* 8, South African Institute of Race Relations, March–July 1989

5 *The Star* 10 January 1990

6 Mashabela H, *Townships of the PWV*, South African Institute of Race Relations, 1988

II Mekhukhu: seven case studies

1 Mashabela H, *Townships of the PWV*, South African Institute of Race Relations, 1988, p97

2 *Sowetan* 10 November 1989

3 Mashabela H, *Townships of the PWV*, South African Institute of Race Relations, 1988, p161

4 *The Star* 6 June 1989

5 Mashabela H, *Townships of the PWV*, South African Institute of Race Relations, 1988, p148

6 *The Star* 18 August 1989

7 Ibid 14 November 1989

8 *Sowetan* 14 April 1989

9 Budlender G, 'Urban Land Issues in the 1980s: The View From Weiler's Farm', unpublished paper delivered at a conference at the University of Cape Town, 18 April 1989

10 Board Notice 85 of 1987, *Government Gazette* 31 December 1987

11 Budlender G, op cit

III Shack settlements and organisation

1 *Sowetan* 19 December 1989

The South African Institute of Race Relations is a non-profitmaking organisation seeking to foster non-violent processes of change towards democracy in South Africa. It has no party political affiliations. Membership is open to all, irrespective of race, colour, creed, nationality, or country of residence.

The occasional publications listed elsewhere in this book are supplemented by *Quarterly Countdown* and *Social and Economic Update* (published every four months) and the annual *Race Relations Survey.*

If you would like to join the Institute and/or receive regular copies of our publications please write to the Membership Manager, South African Institute of Race Relations, P O Box 31044, 2017 Braamfontein.